ELAN GARONZIK

D1190542

THE WHISTLING SKELETON
American Indian Tales of the Supernatural

THE WHISTLING SKELETON
American Indian Tales of the Supernatural

Collected by George Bird Grinnell

Edited by John Bierhorst

Illustrated by Robert Andrew Parker

Four Winds Press · New York

Library of Congress Cataloging in Publication Data

Main entry under title:

The whistling skeleton.

Bibliography: p.
Summary: Includes nine mystery tales told by
Pawnee, Blackfoot, and Cheyenne storytellers in
the late nineteenth century.
1. Indians of North America — Great Plains — Legends.
[1. Indians of North America — Great Plains — Legends.
2. Supernatural — Fiction]   I. Grinnell, George Bird,
1849 – 1938.   II. Bierhorst, John.
E78.G73W43   398.2'08997078   81-69517
ISBN 0-590-07801-1   AACR2

Published by Four Winds Press
A division of Scholastic Inc., New York, N.Y.
Copyright © 1982 by John Bierhorst
All rights reserved
Printed in the United States of America
Library of Congress Catalog Card Number: 81-69517
Book design by Jane Byers Bierhorst
1 2 3 4 5 86 85 84 83 82

CONTENTS

Foreword

In the words of George Bird Grinnell, tales like these were "mystery" stories — stories that contradict the expected turn of events, luring the listener into a world where all things are possible. Many of the stories were told only at night. And if an especially mysterious tale were about to be heard, someone might get up and tie the door shut before the storyteller began.

Outsiders were seldom present at such storytelling sessions. But to the people who related these tales Grinnell was a friend, almost a brother. During the 1870s he had come to know the

Pawnee intimately, living with them in their villages and joining them in their buffalo hunts. In the 1880s he befriended the Blackfeet and, in the 1890s, the Cheyenne. Year after year he returned to these tribes, sharing their experiences, learning to understand the languages they spoke, and listening to their stories.

Although Indian stories had been collected earlier, notably by Henry Rowe Schoolcraft in the 1820s and 1830s, Grinnell was the first to take down these tales in the straightforward, unornamented style that preserves the spirit of the original storytelling performance. It was Grinnell who first gave the Indian narrator an authentic voice in English.

The tales selected for this volume are from the tribes that Grinnell knew best, the Pawnee of Kansas and Nebraska, the Blackfeet of Montana and southern Saskatchewan, and the Cheyenne of Wyoming, Colorado, and western Nebraska. These were people whose livelihood depended upon the great herds of buffalo that roamed the prairies and who counted their wealth in the number of horses they owned. They were proud, warlike, and deeply religious. On the windswept hills and along the streams and rivers they heard the voices of animal spirits and felt the presence of ghosts.

But although the stories told by these tribes often dealt with the supernatural, they also reflected the real world in which the people lived, preserving accurate details about marriage customs, hunting methods, warfare, treatment of the sick, child rearing, and homelife. In the story "The Whistling Skeleton," for example, the skin lodge, or tepee, with its smoke hole and wing flaps, can be quite fully visualized as the people crowd together inside it, trying to protect themselves from a marauding ghost. Earlier in the same story the ghost is said to be wrapped in a lodge cover, just as the body of a deceased person was in fact often wrapped as part of the normal funeral procedure.

Generally speaking, the lodge was the home of a single family. But as several of the stories make clear, the old-style family was not the same as it is today. Once a man had settled down with his first wife, he might take a second and even a third. Multiple marriages are mentioned in the tale called "Wolf Man," in "Red Robe's Dream," and in "Deer Boy."

Before he could marry, however, a young man had to prove himself in war. When he had made several war expeditions, or "warpaths," taking horses from the enemy each time, he might then have enough horses to purchase a bride, making the payment to her father. Among the Cheyenne, if a young couple fell in love and eloped without making payment, it was said that the bride had been "stolen." Against this background the tale called "The Stolen Girl" takes on an added meaning. The usual procedure is exemplified in the story "Sees in the Night."

It should not be assumed that women sat idly to one side, waiting for men to take the initiative. On the contrary, women put pressure on men to go to war and bring home wealth. "Do something great. Then perhaps it will not be useless if you ask my father to give me to you," says the heroine in "Red Robe's Dream." Sometimes the young men were actually taunted, suffering personal insults and accusations of cowardice.

Good looks were helpful in winning a woman. To improve their appearance, young Blackfeet men — not women — spent hours brushing, braiding, and ornamenting their hair. Often they would paint their faces and parade around the camp on their horses, hoping to impress the opposite sex. In "The Death of Low Horn" it is said that the hero was sufficiently good-looking to do without face paint. In fact he thought it was "silly" for a person to paint himself. To the native audience this must have conjured up the image of an unusually handsome boy.

For a man to be rejected by a woman was a serious matter. In the story called "Deer Boy" the hero's father is so ashamed at having been abandoned by his wife that he separates from his tribe, not returning until he has proven himself with great deeds.

On the warpath a man sought to take horses or other valuables and to establish his reputation for bravery by either killing an enemy or counting *coup*. A *coup*, or "strike," could be counted by touching an enemy in battle or by touching the body of an enemy who had just fallen. In this way the warrior exposed himself to great danger. (Even a fallen enemy might suddenly spring up and shoot.) In "Deer Boy" the hero's father counts *coup* on a Comanche that he himself has killed. In "The Death of Low Horn" the hero stands by after killing a Cree and allows his companions to count *coup*. To gain greater speed a warrior might sometimes remove all his clothing and go into battle naked. This curious custom plays a part in "The Death of Low Horn" near the beginning of the story and again at the end.

After a war party returned to camp there might be "feasting." Men would invite each other into their lodges and serve dishes of choice food, perhaps boiled tongue or roasted ribs. While they ate and smoked, they recalled their exploits. Sometimes a man or woman known to be a good storyteller would be called in to entertain the guests. Feasting is mentioned in "The Stolen Girl" and, more fully, in "The Whistling Skeleton."

Although it would appear that every boy was expected to become a warrior, there were, nevertheless, exceptions to this rule. If a young man had a special gift for communicating with the spirits, he might become a medicine man, or doctor. In the story called "The Boy Who Was Sacrificed," such a young man acquires secret knowledge from the "medicine animals" who live beneath a whirlpool in the river. When he returns, he is able to perform the rituals that will heal wounds and cure disease. This tale, incidentally, comes from the Pawnee, the only Indian tribe north of Mexico to have practiced human sacrifice. However, Pawnee sacrifice was an elaborate, public ceremony. It was never performed privately and never by fathers on their own sons, as in this purely fictional story.

The usual method of communicating with spirits was through dreaming. A dead relative or a mysterious animal might appear in a dream, singing a song that the dreamer could later use to gain power over an enemy, find game, or cure sickness. Sometimes special instructions would be given, as in the story "Red Robe's Dream."

Troublesome spirits could be pacified with a gift, or offering, especially a pipe filled with tobacco for the spirit to smoke (as in the final scene of "The Whistling Skeleton").

In almost any situation a person could increase his spiritual power by repeating a song, a saying, or an action exactly four times. The number seven, on the other hand, could bring bad luck or even death. When the narrator mentions that Low Horn's war party was made up of seven men, he seems to be saying that death lies ahead. Similarly, when the men return to camp in "The Whistling Skeleton" and find that there are exactly seven lodges, we can be sure that trouble is in the offing.

A story that is especially rich in American Indian "mystery" is the little tale called "Ghost Story." Although it might not seem so at first glance, this strange narrative is as perfectly constructed as a mathematical formula. In its first half it moves steadily forward. Then it stops, turns backward, and in its second half retraces its steps until it returns to the starting point. In the first half there is a passage through death, represented by the stopover at the ghosts' lodge. In the second half there is also a brush with death, represented by the descent into the mysterious valley where the old woman lives. But while in the first half there is a movement toward adulthood and even a hint that the heroine will take a husband, in the second half she hides the fact that she is now a woman, dresses as a man, rejects the advances of the opposite sex, and returns to the scene of her childhood.

Such a story is really more than a mere tale. It is a subtle myth about growing up. What it suggests is that the child within you must die if you are to become an adult — this much is accomplished by the first half of the story. But to keep on living you must preserve the child, or at least a part of the child, that you once were. And it is for this reason that the heroine retraces her steps until at the end she seems to be a child all over again, while of course remaining an adult. The double route she follows, forward and backward, is actually the plot of the story — and precisely the same plot that is found in a great many Indian myths from all parts of North America.

As a further question, it would be interesting to ask: Who were the tellers of these stories? What were their names? Were they mostly men, or women? In recent years folklorists have discovered that it often makes a difference whether the teller is male or female. A woman, for example, may take a story that is usually told by men and turn it around so that the hero becomes a heroine. And men, not surprisingly, may do just the opposite. War stories are typically, though not always, told by men, while stories that deal with marriage are often, but again not always, favored by women.

In Grinnell's day the study of folklore was just beginning, and collectors for the most part never thought to record the names of storytellers. In fact it was widely believed that folktales were handed down unchanged from generation to generation. As we now know, this is not true.

Nevertheless, Grinnell did record the names of his principal Pawnee informant and several of his Blackfeet informants, and while he did not pass on the names of any Cheyenne story-tellers, he recorded the important information that they included both men and women. From such clues as we have, it may be stated with a fair degree of certainty that the two Pawnee stories "Deer Boy" and "The Boy Who Was Sacrificed" were told in 1888 by the warrior White Eagle, also known as Eagle Chief. Among Grinnell's Blackfeet informants, all of them male, were Red Eagle, Almost-a-Dog, Heavy Runner, All-Are-His-Children, and Lone Medicine Person. Unfortunately, Grinnell does not say which tales were obtained from which informants. In addition, he obtained a number of Black-feet stories from the collector J.W. Schultz, some of whose informants may have been women. Almost certainly a tale like "The Death of Low Horn" was obtained from a man. But it would be difficult to say for sure whether "Red Robe's Dream" or even "Sees in the Night" had been told by a man or a woman.

Very likely the Cheyenne story called "The Stolen Girl" came from a female informant. And the subtle "Ghost Story" — perhaps the most mysterious tale in the present collection — might well have been told by a woman.

Grinnell himself, though best known today for his studies of

Indian culture, began his career as a zoologist. While earning his doctorate at Yale University in the mid-1870s, he regularly joined summer collecting expeditions to the Missouri River country, the Black Hills, and the Northern Rockies. A specialist in birds and mammals, he was also a sportsman and a conservationist. In the late 1870s he was instrumental in securing legislation to protect Yellowstone National Park, and it was largely due to his efforts that Glacier National Park was established in 1910. During these years he became widely known as the editor of the sportsman's weekly, *Forest and Stream,* later called *Field and Stream.* In 1902 he married Elizabeth Curtis Williams, who thereafter accompanied him on his western expeditions, becoming his official photographer. A lifelong resident of New York City, he died in 1938 at the age of eighty-eight.

Throughout his long career he remained loyal to the three Indian tribes he had befriended during his earlier years, the Pawnee, the Blackfeet, and especially the Cheyenne, whom he visited every year up into the 1920s. Owing to his prolonged personal contact with these tribes, he was able to write about them with the kind of authority that few non-Indians could match. Moreover, in his numerous books and articles on Indian history and customs, he typically allowed his Indian informants to speak for themselves. As for his folklore collections, these set new standards of taste and accuracy that were to be continually copied by later investigators; and although twentieth-century folklorists, especially with the aid of the phonograph and the tape recorder, have been able to improve upon his methods, it is fair to say that Grinnell—with his deep commitment to pre-serving a record of Indian life as it truly was lived and with his keen ear for Indian speech—was the first modern collector of native American short stories.

J.B.

West Shokan, N.Y.
December 1980

THE WHISTLING SKELETON
American Indian Tales of the Supernatural

The Whistling Skeleton

The people were camped at Old Man's River, where Fort McLeod now stands. A party of seven men started to war toward the Cypress Hills. Heavy Collar was the leader. They went around the Hills but found no enemies and started back toward camp. On the way home Heavy Collar took the lead. He would go out far ahead and look over the country, acting as scout for the party. After a while they came to the south branch of the Saskatchewan River, above Seven Persons' Creek. In those days there was always a danger of being surprised by enemies, and so these men traveled concealed as much as possible in the ravines and low places.

As they were going up the river, they saw three old bulls in the distance, lying close to a cut bank. Heavy Collar left his party and went out to kill one of these bulls, and when he got close enough, he shot one and killed it right there. He cut it up, and, being hungry, he went down into a ravine to roast a piece of the meat. He had left his party a long way behind, and night was now coming on.

As he was roasting the meat, he began to feel very tired, and he thought, "It's too bad I didn't bring along one of my young men. He could go up on that hill and get some hair from that bull's head, and I could wipe out my gun."

While he sat there talking to himself this way, a bunch of hair from the buffalo's head came flying through the air and fell on the ground right in front of him. It scared him a little. Who could have done this? He wondered if there were enemies close by. After a little while he picked up the hair and cleaned his gun and loaded it. Then he sat and watched to see if anyone was coming.

He was uneasy and finally decided he would go on up the river to see what he could discover. He went on upstream until he came to the mouth of the St. Mary's River. It was now late at night, and he was tired, so he crept into a patch of rye grass to hide and sleep for the night.

The summer before, a woman had been killed in this same patch of grass where Heavy Collar lay down to rest. He did not know this. But still he was troubled that night. He couldn't sleep. He kept hearing something, but he couldn't make out what it was.

Again and again he tried to sleep, but every time he dozed off he kept thinking he heard something in the distance. The next morning, when it was light, he saw right there beside him the skeleton of the woman who had been killed the summer before.

He went on, continuing upstream to Belly River. But all day as he was traveling he kept thinking about having slept next to that woman's bones. It bothered him. He could not forget it. At the same time he was very tired, because he had walked so far and had slept so little.

When it began to get dark, he crossed over to an island and decided to camp for the night. At the upper end of the island there was a large tree that had drifted down and got caught, and in a fork of this tree he built his fire. Then he got in between one of the forks and sat with his back to the fire, warming himself. But all the time he was thinking about the bones he had slept next to the night before.

All of a sudden he heard a sound as if something were being dragged toward him along the ground. It sounded as if a piece of a lodge were being dragged over the grass. It came closer and closer.

Heavy Collar was scared. He was afraid to turn his

head and look back to see what it was. He heard the noise come up to the tree where he had his fire. Then it stopped, and all at once he heard someone whistling a tune.

He turned around and looked. And there, sitting on another fork of the tree, right across from him, was the pile of bones he'd slept next to the night before, only now all together in the shape of a skeleton.

The skeleton was wrapped in a lodge covering. And the string that usually hangs from one of the lodge poles was tied around the skeleton's neck. The wings of the lodge stood out on either side of her head, and behind her the lodge could be seen stretching out and fading away into the darkness. She sat on an old dead limb and whistled her tune, and as she whistled, she swung her legs in time to the tune.

When Heavy Collar saw this, his heart almost melted away. At last he got up his courage and said, "Ghost, go away. Don't bother me. I'm very tired. I want to rest."

The ghost paid no attention, but kept on whistling, swinging her legs in time to the tune. Four times he prayed to her, saying, "Ghost, take pity on me. Go away and leave me alone. I'm tired. I want to rest."

But the more he prayed, the more the ghost whistled and seemed pleased, swinging her legs and turning her head from side to side, sometimes looking down at him and sometimes up at the stars, and all the time whistling.

When he saw that she paid no attention to what he was saying, Heavy Collar got angry in his heart. "Ghost, you do not listen to my prayers," he said, "and so I will have to shoot you to make you go away." And with that he reached for his gun, and, throwing it to his shoulder, shot right at the ghost.

As he fired, she fell over backward into the darkness, screaming out, "O Heavy Collar, you've shot me, you've killed me! You dog, Heavy Collar! There is no place on this earth where you can go that I will not find you, no place where you can hide that I will not come."

As she fell back and said this, Heavy Collar jumped

to his feet and ran away as fast as he could. She called after him, "I have been killed once, and now you are trying to kill me again. O Heavy Collar!"

As he ran away, he could still hear her angry words following him, until at last they died away in the distance. He ran all night long, and whenever he stopped to breathe and listen, he seemed to hear in the distance the echo of her voice. All he could hear was, "O Heavy Collar!" and then he would rush away again.

He ran until he was all tired out, and by this time it was daylight. He was now quite a long way below Fort McLeod. He was very sleepy but didn't dare stop for fear the ghost would catch up to him. He kept walking on for a long time, and when he finally did sit down to rest, he fell asleep immediately.

Now, before he had left his men, Heavy Collar had said to them, "Remember, anybody who gets separated from the rest of us should always go to the Belly River Buttes. That will be our meeting place."

So when their leader did not return, the party started

cross country toward the Belly River Buttes.

Heavy Collar had followed the river a long distance out of his way, and when he awoke from his sleep, he too started straight for the Belly River Buttes, just as he had said he would.

When the party got to the Buttes, one of the men went up on top to watch. After a while, looking down the river, he saw two people coming, and as they got closer, he saw that one of them was Heavy Collar, and by his side was a woman. The watcher called the rest of the party to come up. "Look!" he said. "There's our chief. He's had good luck. He's bringing a woman with him. If he brings her into camp we'll take her away from him." And they all laughed. They thought he had captured her.

They went back down to the campsite and sat around the fire, watching the two people who were coming toward them, and laughing among themselves at the idea of their chief bringing in a woman.

When the two got close, the young men could see that Heavy Collar was walking fast, and the woman would walk by his side a little way, trying to keep up, and then fall behind and trot along to catch up again. Just before the pair reached camp there was a deep ravine they had to cross. They went down into it, side by side, and then Heavy Collar came up out of it alone and walked on into the camp.

When he got there, all the young men began to laugh at him, and they called out, "Heavy Collar, where is your woman?" He looked at them for a moment and then said, "I have no woman. I don't know what you're talking about."

Then one of them said, "He's hiding her in that ravine. He's afraid to bring her into camp." Another said, "Where did you capture her, and what tribe does she belong to?"

Heavy Collar looked at first one and then another and said, "I think you are all crazy. I've taken no woman. What do you mean?"

"That woman you had with you just now. Where did you get her, and where did you put her? Isn't she down there in that ravine? We all saw her. It's no use pretending she wasn't with you. Come on, now, where is she?"

When they said this, Heavy Collar's heart grew very heavy. He knew that it must have been the ghost woman. Then he told them the story. Some of the young men would not believe it, and they ran down to the ravine, where they had last seen the woman. In the soft dirt they saw the tracks made by Heavy Collar, but there were no other tracks near his, where they had seen the woman walking. Then they realized it was a ghost that had been following him.

By this time the party had been gone so long that their moccasins were all worn out, and they decided they had better go back to their home camp. They could not travel fast because some of them had sore feet. But at last they came to the cut banks that they recognized, and there they found their camp — exactly seven lodges.

That night they invited each other to feasts, and

someone called out to Heavy Collar, asking him to come eat with him. Heavy Collar shouted, "Yes, I will be there shortly." But already it was getting late, and the moon was bright.

Heavy Collar got up and went out of his lodge, walked a little way, then sat down to rest a moment. While he was sitting, a big bear came out of the brush right next to him. He felt around for a stone to throw at it to scare it away, thinking it hadn't seen him. As he was feeling the earth, his hand hit a piece of bone, and he picked it up and threw it at the bear and hit it. Then the bear spoke: "Heavy Collar! First you kill me, and now you're hitting me. Is there any place in this world where you can hide from me? Go where you like. I will always find you."

When Heavy Collar heard this, he knew it was the ghost woman, and he jumped up and ran back to his lodge, crying, "Everybody run! There's a ghost bear!"

Then they all ran into Heavy Collar's lodge, and it was crowded with people. There was a big fire in the lodge, and the wind was blowing hard from the west. Men, women, and children were huddled together inside, all very much afraid of the ghost. They could hear her walking toward them, grumbling, and saying, "I'll kill these dogs. Not one of them will get away."

She kept coming closer and closer, until she was right at the lodge door. Then she said, "I'll smoke you to death!" And with these words she moved the poles so that the wings of the lodge turned toward the west and the wind could blow in through the smoke hole. All the while, she was threatening them with terrible things. The lodge began to get full of smoke, the children were crying, and everybody was choking. Then they said, "Let's lift up one man and have him fix the ears so the lodge will get clear of smoke." Then they raised him up on their shoulders, and, blinded and half strangled by the smoke, he tried to turn the wings.

But just at that moment the ghost hit the lodge and said, "*Unh!*" And the people who were holding the man were so frightened that they jumped and let him go, and he fell down. Then the people didn't know what to do, and they said, "It's no use. She's determined to smoke us to death." And all the while the smoke was getting thicker in the lodge.

"Is it possible that she can destroy us?" asked Heavy Collar. "Is there no one here who has some strong dream power that can overcome this ghost?"

Then his mother said, "I will try to do something. I am older than any of you, and I will see what I can do to save you." So she got down her medicine bundle and painted herself, and got out a pipe and filled it with tobacco and lighted it, and sat there and began to pray to the ghost woman. She said, "Ghost, take pity on us, and go away. Save these people. We have never hurt you. Why are you threatening us and frightening our children? Accept what I offer you, and leave us alone."

A voice came from behind the lodge and said, "No, I will not listen to you. Every one of you must die, you dogs!"

The old woman repeated her prayer: "Ghost, take

pity on us. Save us. Accept this tobacco and go away."

Then the ghost said, "How can you expect me to smoke, when I am way back here? Bring me the pipe. I'm not long enough to reach around the lodge." So the old woman went out through the door and held the stem of the pipe as far as she could around toward the back of the lodge.

The ghost said, "No, I will not come get it. If you want me to smoke, you must bring it here."

Then the old woman went closer, and the ghost began to back away, saying, "No, I do not smoke that kind of pipe." But when the ghost started away, the old woman followed her. She was drawn to the ghost. She could not help herself.

She called out, "Oh, my children, the ghost is carrying me off!" Heavy Collar rushed out and called to the others, "Come, help me pull my mother away from the ghost." He grasped his mother around the waist and held her, and another man took him by the waist, and another him, until they were all strung out, one behind the other, all following the old woman, who was following the ghost.

All at once the old woman let go of the pipe and fell over dead. The ghost disappeared, the wind died down, the children stopped crying, and the people were saved.

Sees in the Night

The camp was moving, but every stream they came to was dry. They could find no water. They kept on until they reached a creek where they found water by digging holes, and here they camped. The next day they moved on and set out for the big river. At the camp, they left behind an old dog with a litter of puppies. The people came to the big river and crossed it and went up on the other side.

A poor boy who had no home crossed with the rest, and when they had come out of the river he lay down under a tree and went to sleep. The dog with her puppies was following up the trail of the camp. In his sleep the boy heard the dog coming, singing. It sounded like a young woman singing. She sang a song twice over, and after each song she stopped and howled four times like a wolf.

The dog kept coming closer and closer, singing the same song. Then she began to sing another song different from the first, and again she howled four times like a wolf.

At last she spoke. "Do not harm my children," she said. "Take pity on my children. Carry them across the river." After that she sang another song, the same as before, and howled four times and spoke again, saying, "*Wu hu is tat' tan,* do not harm my children. Take pity on my children. Carry them across the river safely. I know that you are a poor boy and have no father. You have no home. You are on the prairie. I know the man road and the war trail. I am a woman. I know the woman trail. If you carry my children across safely, I will take pity on you and help you."

The boy was very poor. He had only an old worn-out robe, and every part of his clothing was bad. When he heard the dog coming, he got up and looked across the river, and when he saw her, he held up both hands. He wanted the dog to take pity on him.

When the dog reached the river bank, the boy waded over to meet her and took two of the puppies and carried them over, and then went back again and took over two more, and then again, and took the last two. As he was carrying over the last two, the mother jumped in and swam across. When she had reached the other side she said to the boy, "Where is the camp?"

"It is right below here," he said. "Right around that bend. Look, there are some of the people coming out in small groups. I think they are going to hunt buffalo."

The dog spoke again to the boy. "I know that you have no home," she said, "and therefore I am going to take pity on you. Look at your moccasins and your robe. They are full of holes. But you shall not always be poor. You shall have a name, and your name shall be known everywhere. You shall have friends, and you shall have relatives. I am a woman, and I know that you shall have relatives. Two or three or four days after a war party starts, you must follow it, and you must sing these songs that you have heard me sing.

"You must do just as I tell you," she said. "You must start out two or three or four days after the war party has left. That's when you must go, even if you have to start at night. If you go at night it will be just the same to you as day, and you will be able to follow the trail."

The dog went on to the camp. After she had gone a little way, the boy saw an old woman coming. She took up the puppies and carried them on. The people were about to go out on a buffalo hunt.

The boy told no one what the dog had said to him. He kept it a secret. At night he would go out into the hills and cry and pray for help and good luck. In time, he grew up to be a young man. A war party was about to start, and he thought to himself, "I wonder if that dog told me the truth."

He decided to wait three days before following the trail of the war party. He had said he would join it, and after it had started, people began to ask him when he was going to leave. To those who questioned him, he answered, "I will be leaving in a little while."

Three days after the war party had started, he followed it. That night he camped. The next day he went on, following the trail. Night came again, but this time he traveled in the dark, singing the songs the dog had sung, and to him the darkness was like daylight. He could see the buffalo on each side of the trail.

The third night he traveled again, singing the songs the dog had taught him, and after each song he howled like a wolf, four times. The following night, about the middle of the night, he came to the camp of the war party. Some of the people were still awake, and when he reached the camp they called him to the war lodge to which he belonged. A man said to him, "We had been expecting you, but finally we thought you were not coming."

"Oh," he said, "I thought I would wait about three days before starting."

The next morning they went on, but it was three or four days before they found the Crow camp. When they reached it, they waited until night so that they could take horses. Then they separated to look for the horses.

The young man and another young man whom he knew well went together. He said to his friend, "Let us go this way." No one knew that he could see as well by night as by day.

They came to a bunch of horses and he said to his friend, "You take these, and I will go across and see if I can find some more." Across the stream he could see another bunch of horses. He picked out the ones he wanted and brought them all back to the home camp. Then he helped the people who had taken care of him when he was little by giving them some of these horses.

After that, whenever a war party was starting out,

there were always young men who wanted to remain behind and go with him. They wanted to see what he did on his journey. They were trying to find out about him.

They started on another war party, and two or three stayed behind to go with him. After the party had started, these young men kept urging him to start, saying, "We do not believe that you are going." But he said, "Wait, we will catch up to them."

When they started, he taught these young men his songs, and they did just as he did. They took many horses. When they came home, the chief of the camp said, "I would like to have that young man for my son-in-law." When the people he lived with heard this, they sent horses for the girl, and he married her.

Now he was rich and had a big skin lodge and plenty of friends and plenty of relatives. He was made a chief. He never had any bad luck. He always had good luck on his warpaths. Everything the dog had told him came true.

Deer Boy

Once when the tribe was on its summer hunt, a long time ago, a man and his wife got into an argument. They had a child, a boy about ten months old. It was while they were traveling along, going from one camp to another, that they began to argue. At last the wife became furious and threw the baby at the man and said, "You take this baby. It's a man child, so it belongs to you. I'm not going to nurse it for you any longer." Then she went away.

The man took the child and carried it along with him. He felt very badly, both for himself and for his child. He was so unhappy that he almost wanted to kill himself. He felt ashamed that he, being a man, should be made to take care of his child, because he had no female relatives who could take care of it for him. He was so ashamed that he decided to leave the tribe and wander off alone, far from his people.

So he went away, carrying the child on his back as a woman does. When it cried for its mother's milk, he had none to give it. He could only cry with it. He hated to kill the child or to leave it behind to die on the prairie. So he wandered off to the south and kept traveling, until at last he came to where the buffalo were.

By this time, the child had changed from a very fat baby to a very thin one, because it had not been nursed. When the man got to the buffalo, he killed a cow and took its udder, and while it was fresh, he let the child suck it until it was sour. Then he killed another cow and did the same thing.

Sometimes he would get a slice of meat and half cook it and let the child suck the juice. In this way, the man kept the child alive, and at last it got used to this food and became strong and well. By this time the man had gone a long way.

After a while, he found that the child could sit up alone. Then he began to give the boy all sorts of things to play with. First he made him a little bow and some arrows and taught him how to use them. He made other things, too, so that the child would be able to play alone. Then the father would go off a little way, perhaps to the top of a nearby hill, to look off over the countryside, but he would look back at the boy every few steps to make sure he was all right.

Finally the father went off for half a day, and when he came back he found the child still playing. By this time the boy had begun to walk. Then the father killed a buffalo cow and made some dried meat and told his son to go get a piece whenever he was hungry.

The father now went off and was gone a whole day, and when he came back at night the child was safe. At last he left on a two-day trip, staying overnight and coming back the next day. When he returned, the boy was asleep. A second time he went away and was gone for two days, traveling far. When he came back, he found that the child was painted with white clay. The father thought this was strange. He said to himself, "Something must have come and talked to my child. Something is taking care of him while I am gone."

When he came back the third time after an overnight trip, he found that the child had a string of wild currants around his neck. The fourth long trip he took lasted three days, and when he returned he found his son still wearing the same string of currants, and with a feather tied on his head.

The father now knew that something was looking after his child, and when he went off he would pray for the child. He would say, "Ho! Whatever it is that is taking pity on my child, also take pity on me!"

About this time the boy was getting old enough to talk, and one day he said, "Father, go off and stay for four days. I will be all right. When you come back you will find me safe."

The man went. He started to go south, far south, because now he would be gone for four days. When he had been gone two days and two nights, he saw a signal smoke and went toward it. Peeking over a hill, he saw many horses and people coming down toward a river.

He lay on the hill a long time, watching to see where they would camp. When they had made camp, he went into a ravine and crept closer. After a while, he could see that there was just one lodge and that all around it was a whole herd of horses. He waited until after dark and then went up to the lodge.

The lodge was surrounded by horses. Everywhere nothing but horses, there were so many. He crept closer and looked in through an opening by the door. Inside he could see a great big man and two women — only three people in all. He thought he recognized one of the women. He kept looking at her, and at last he remembered who she was and that she had been captured long ago from his tribe. Her people were still living.

While he was watching, the man inside the lodge asked for something, and the captive woman stood up to go outside. As the woman came out into the darkness and went among the horses, the man who had been watching stepped up behind her very softly, put his hand on her shoulder, and said to her in her own language, "Friend, do you belong to my tribe?"

The woman started to scream, but he put his hand on her mouth and said to her, "Be quiet. Keep still. Do not call out." She answered him, "Yes, I belong to your tribe."

Then he asked her, "Who is that other woman I see in the lodge?" She answered him, "She also belongs to our tribe and is a prisoner." Then the man said, "You wait and keep still. I am going to kill that man."

The woman said, "That is good. This man is the biggest man of all the Comanches. He has come to this place ahead of the others. The rest of the Comanches are going to meet him here. Do not fail to kill him. I will tell the other woman that our friend is here, and we will wait and watch."

When the woman went into the lodge, she whispered to the other woman, "Be ready. A friend who belongs to our tribe is here. Take your hatchet and be prepared to help kill our husband."

The two women waited, and the man got ready to shoot the Comanche with his bow and arrow. The woman had said to him, "Push aside the door a little and wait for the right moment." He made a small opening by the door, just big enough to let an arrow pass through, and when the time came he let it go.

U'-ra-rish! The arrow flew straight. It pierced the Comanche through the heart, and he died. Then the man counted *coup* on him and took his scalp.

The women felt so glad to meet a friend that they put their arms around the man and patted him. Now they would be going back home to see their relatives. They asked him, "How many of you are here?" He answered, "I am alone." They were surprised.

They took down the lodge, packed everything on the horses, and drove off the herd, leaving the dead body of the Comanche at the campsite. All night they traveled and all the next day. As they were going along, the women told him that there were about three hundred head of horses in the herd that they had with them. Then the man told them how it happened that he was alone, and the closer they got to where the child had been left, the faster the women ran their horses. When they reached the boy, they picked him up in their arms and petted him, and took him as their own.

Now the father was no longer sad. He had rescued two captured women, had killed an enemy,

and had taken a whole herd of horses.

They went on and traveled far and at last, one night, they came to where the tribe was living and camped with them. The horses completely surrounded the lodge — you could just see the top of it over their backs. The next morning all the people wondered who these strangers could be. Then they found out that the man and child who were lost had returned, and with them two women, captured long ago by the Comanches. Then there was great joy in the tribe.

The man gave his relatives many horses. In those days the people had only a few, and it seems that this man brought good luck in horses to the tribe. Ever since that time they have had many. As for the mother of the boy, when she heard that her child was alive she came running to see him, but she was whipped out of the lodge.

The child grew to be a young man, and he became rich. When he was grown, he told his father that ever since he could remember, a buck deer had talked to him and taken care of him. It was the deer that had saved the boy and brought the father good luck when they were living alone on the prairie. So that the deer would be remembered, the boy established a dance — and this is the deer dance that is still performed today.

The Stolen Girl

There was once a young girl who had many men coming to see her. She was the daughter of a chief, and his lodge was pitched in the center of the circle. Many young men wanted to marry her, but she refused them all. She did not care for any of them. She wanted a young man that she could love.

One evening, as she sat in the lodge, she

noticed a pleasant odor in the air and wondered where it came from. She wanted to look out and see, but she did not want anyone to find her at the door. So she took her mother's awl and punched a hole in the lodge skins. Peering through the hole, she saw a young man standing not far off.

After she had looked at him for a little while, she liked him and decided that she would go out and see who he was. She walked past him, he spoke to her, and she stopped. Then they talked to each other, and the girl asked him who he was and why he had come, because she could see that he was a stranger.

"The home of my people is far from here," he said, "and I have come to get you. Come with me, and we will go to my father's lodge."

The young man spoke beautifully, and the girl, after she had thought a little while, said to him, "Yes, I will go with you. Other young men want me, but I do not want them. I will go only with you. But first you must let me go back and get my awl and sinew and my quills."

She went into the lodge and made up a bundle of her things. Then she came out again and said to the young man, "Now, I am ready. Where do you live from here? Which way do we go?"

"I live toward the rising sun," said the young man. "There are many camps of my people there." And so they set out toward the east.

As they were going along, she said to him, "What is your name? What does the caller call out when you want your friends to come feast with you?"

"My name," he said, "is Red Eye."

They kept on traveling. At last, when it was almost night, they came to the camp. There were many trees where the camp was pitched, and all among the trees they could see the light shining through the lodge skins. They went into the camp circle and up to a big lodge standing in the middle.

When they got to the door, they stopped. Through

the lodge skins they could see the shadows of many men sitting around the fire and could hear them talking and laughing. The young man's father was speaking. He said to the others, "My son has gone far away. He has gone to get a chief's daughter to marry. He has seen her and liked her, and now he has gone to get her. After a while, if he has good luck, he will come back with her." The old man kept on talking about his son.

At last Red Eye said to the girl, "Come, let us go in." Red Eye went first. When his father saw him, he was surprised. He said, "Ah, my son, I did not think I would see you so soon. I hope you have had good luck."

The girl followed the young man into the lodge and went over and sat on the women's side. She saw her father-in-law speaking to her husband, and she noticed that he had a very sharp nose. After a while, looking around, she saw that all the men in the lodge had sharp noses. The lodge was richly furnished and the linings beautifully painted. On the beds were many fine buffalo robes.

Meanwhile, at the girl's home, there was great worry. The chief's daughter had disappeared, and no one knew what had become of her. Her father and mother were crying because their daughter was lost. All the young men were out looking for her. But they could not find her or any trace of her.

Seeing that the search was coming to nothing, the father felt still worse, and he said to the young men who had been out looking, "The man who finds my daughter shall marry her."

Now, when the girl woke up the next morning, she found herself in a big hollow tree, and sitting all around her were mountain rats. The buffalo robes on which they had been lying were grass nests.

Just then, a young man who was out looking for the lost girl happened to be passing this hollow tree, and as he passed by, he saw the girl come crawling out.

"Young woman," he said, "where have you been? People at home are crying because you are lost. We have been looking for you everywhere."

"Friend," said the girl, "I was stolen by rats. They brought me here to this tree." (And that, they say, was the beginning of rats stealing things from people.) Then the young man took her back to her father's lodge, and before long they were married.

The Death of Low Horn

I

In the Blackfeet camp many years ago there lived a boy named Screech Owl. He was a lonely boy who liked to be by himself. Often he would stay away from camp all night, and he would pray to all kinds of birds and animals and ask them to take pity on him and help him, saying that he wanted to be a warrior. He never used paint. He was a good-looking boy, and he thought it was silly for a person to paint himself.

When Screech Owl was about fourteen, a large party of Blackfeet was starting to war against the Crees. The boy said to his father, "Many of my cousins are joining this war party. I think I am old enough to go with them."

"My son," said the father, "I am willing. You may go."

Then the father gave his son his own war horse, a black horse with a white spot on its side—a very fast horse. And he offered him weapons. But the boy refused them all, except for a little trapping axe. He said, "I think this hatchet will be all that I need."

Just as they were about to start, the father gave the boy his own war headdress. This was not a war bonnet but a plume made of small feathers, the feathers of thunderbirds, because the thunderbird was the father's medicine. The father said to the boy, "My son, when you go into battle, put this plume on your head and wear it as I have worn it."

The war party started out, traveling northeast. After a long while they came to the Saskatchewan River, where they saw three riders, going out hunting. These riders had not seen the war party. The Blackfeet stopped and made plans to go around them and head them off. While they were stopped, Screech Owl got down from his horse, took off all his clothes, put on his father's war plume, and began to ride around, singing his father's war song.

The older warriors were getting ready for the attack, and when they saw this young boy riding around, they thought he was making fun of the older men, and they said, "Look at this boy. He has no shame. He had better stay behind."

When they were ready to go, they told him to wait. Then they started off to charge the Crees. But the boy, instead of waiting behind, charged with them and took the lead—he had the best horse of all. He, a boy, was leading the war party and still singing his war song.

The three Crees began to run, and the boy kept gaining on them. They did not want to separate, they kept together, and the boy pulled closer and closer. Then the last one turned in his saddle and shot, but missed. As the Cree fired, the boy whipped up his horse, rode alongside the Cree, and struck him with his little trapping axe and knocked him off his horse.

Screech Owl paid no attention to the man he had struck, but rode on to the next Cree. As he came up even with him, the Cree raised his gun and fired, but just then the boy dropped down on the other side of his horse, and the ball passed over him. He straightened up on his horse again, rode up beside the Cree, and as he passed, knocked him off his horse with his axe. When he knocked the second Cree off his horse, the Blackfeet, who were following, whooped in triumph and encouraged him, shouting, *A-wa-heh'.*" The boy was still singing his father's war song.

By this time, the main body of the Blackfeet were catching up with him. He whipped his horse on both sides, and rode on after the third Cree, who was also whipping his horse as hard as he could, trying to get away. Meanwhile, some of the Blackfeet had stopped to count *coup* and scalp the two dead Crees and catch the two horses.

At last Screech Owl got close to the third Cree, who kept aiming his gun at him. The boy did not want to get too near until the Cree had fired, but he was gaining a little, and all the time he was throwing himself from side to side on his horse to make it harder for the Cree to hit him. Finally the Cree turned, raised his gun, and fired. But the boy had thrown himself down behind his horse, and again the ball passed over him. He raised himself up on his horse, rushed on the Cree, and struck him in the side of the body with his axe, and then again. And with the second blow he knocked him off his horse.

The boy rode on a little further, stopped, and jumped

off his horse, while the rest of the Blackfeet were coming up and killing the fallen man. He stood off to one side and watched them count *coup* and scalp the dead.

The Blackfeet were surprised at what the young man had done. After a little while, the leader decided they would go back to camp. When they had returned, the boy's name was changed from Screech Owl to Low Horn. This was his first warpath.

From that time on, the name of Low Horn was often heard as that of one doing some great deed.

II

Low Horn started on his last warpath from the Blackfeet crossing. He led a party of six. He was the seventh man.

On the second day out, they came to Red Deer's River. When they reached this river, they found it very high, so they built a raft to cross on. They camped on the other side. In crossing, most of their powder got wet.

The next morning, when they awoke, Low Horn said, "Trouble is coming. We had better turn back. We started on a bad day. In my sleep I saw our bodies lying on the prairie, dead."

Some of the young men said, "We have started, we had better go on. Perhaps it is only a mistake. Let us go on and try to take some horses anyway."

"True," said Low Horn, "it would be silly to try nothing. But remember that it is by your wish that we are going on." He wanted to go back not on his own account but for the sake of his men — to save his followers.

From there they went on and made another camp, and the next morning he said to his men, "Now I am sure. I have seen it for certain. Trouble is coming."

They camped two nights at this place and dried some of their powder, but most of it was caked and spoiled. Low Horn said to his men, "Look. We have no ammunition. We cannot defend ourselves. Let us turn back from here." So they started cross-country for home.

When they reached Red Deer's River, they camped there again. The next morning Low Horn said, "I feel very uneasy today. Two of you go ahead on the trail and keep a close lookout. I am afraid that today we are going to see our enemy."

Two of the young men went ahead, and when they had climbed to the top of a ridge and looked over it on to Saskatoon Creek, they came back and told Low Horn that they had seen a large camp of people and that they thought it was the Blackfeet, who had all moved over there together. Saskatoon Creek was about twenty miles from the Blackfeet camp.

Low Horn said, "No, it cannot be our people. They said nothing about moving over here. It must be a war party."

But the two young men said, "Yes, they are our people. There are too many of them for a war party. We think the whole camp is there."

"Go ahead, then," said Low Horn, "and if you

see my father tell him I will come into the camp to-night. I do not like to come home when I am not bringing anything with me."

It was now late in the afternoon, and the two young men went ahead toward the camp, traveling slowly. A little after sunset they came down the hill to the flat of the creek and saw the camp. They walked down toward it, to the edge of the stream, and there they met two women who had come for water. The men spoke to them in Blackfeet and said, "Is this the Blackfeet camp?"

The women did not understand, so they spoke again. Then the two women called out in the Cree language, "Here are two Blackfeet, coming up and talking to us!"

When the men heard the women talk Cree, and saw the mistake they had made, they turned and ran up the creek. They ran to a place where a few willow bushes were hanging over the stream, a short distance above the camp, and pushing through these, they hid under the bank, and the willows concealed them.

The people in the camp came rushing out, and men ran up the creek and down, looking everywhere for the two enemies. But no one could find them.

Now, while the Crees were running in all directions hunting for these two men, Low Horn was slowly coming down the valley with the four other Blackfeet. He saw men coming toward him and thought they were some of his own people, coming to meet him with horses for him to ride. When they got close, and Low Horn could see that they were the enemy and were taking the covers off their guns, he jumped to one side and stood alone and began to sing his war song. He called out, "Children of the Crees, if you have come to try my manhood, do your best."

In a moment he was surrounded, and they were shooting at him from all directions. He called out again. "People, you can't kill me here. I will take my body to your camp, and only there will you be able to kill me."

He started fighting his way toward the Cree

camp and immediately killed two of the enemy. They kept coming up and clustering around him, some on foot, some on horseback. They were thick on all sides, and they could not get a good shot at him for fear of killing their own people on the other side.

One of the Blackfeet fell. Low Horn said to his men, *"A-wa-heh'!* These people cannot kill us here. We will head for that patch of chokecherry brush, right in the middle of their camp, and there we will take our stand."

Another Blackfeet fell, and now there were only three of them. Low Horn said to his remaining men, "Go straight to that patch of brush. I will fight them off in front and on the sides to keep the way open for you. These Crees cannot kill us here. There are too many of their own people." At last they reached the patch of brush, and with their knives they began to dig dirt and throw up a barrier.

In the Cree camp was *Kom-in'-a-kus,* chief of the Crees, who could talk Blackfeet well. He called out,

"Low Horn, there is a little ravine running out of that brush patch and into the hills. Crawl out that way and try to escape. It is not guarded."

Low Horn answered, "No, children of the Crees, I will not go. Remember, it is Low Horn that you are fighting — a man who has done much harm to your people. I am glad that I am here. I am sorry for only one thing: my powder is going to run out. Tomorrow you may kill me."

All night long, the fighting kept up, the enemy shooting the whole time. And all night long, Low Horn sang his death song. *Kom-in'-a-kus* called to him several times, "Low Horn, you had better do what I tell you. Try to get away." But he shouted back, "No," and laughed at them. He said, "You have killed my men. I am here alone, but you cannot kill me."

Kom-in'-a-kus said, "Well, if you are there when daylight comes, I will go into that brush and catch you with my hands. I will be the one who puts an end to you."

"*Kom-in'-a-kus,* do not try that," said Low Horn. "If you do, you will die." The patch of brush in which he had hidden had now been all shot away, cut to pieces by the bullets of the enemy.

When morning came, Low Horn called out, "*Kom-in'-a-kus,* it is broad daylight now. I have no more powder in my horn. Come and take me with your hands." *Kom-in'-a-kus* answered, "Yes, I said I would catch you, and now I am coming."

He took off all his clothes and rushed over the dirt barrier. Low Horn's powder was all gone, but he still had his knife — and one load in his gun. *Kom-in'-a-kus* came with his gun at his shoulder. Low Horn sat there with his gun in his hand, watching. He was singing his death song. As *Kom-in'-a-kus* got up close, and just as he was about to pull the trigger, Low Horn threw up his gun and fired. The ball knocked off the Cree's forefinger and, going on, entered his right eye and came out at the temple, knocking the eye out. *Kom-in'-a-kus* went down, and his gun flew into the air.

When *Kom-in'-a-kus* fell, the whole camp shouted the war whoop. "That was his last shot," they cried, and they all charged. They knew that Low Horn had no more powder.

The head warrior of the Crees was named Bunch of Lodges. He was the first to jump inside the barrier. As he sprang inside, Low Horn met him and drove his knife through him, killing him on the spot. Then, as the Crees threw themselves over the barrier and he began to feel the knives sticking into him from all sides, he gave a war whoop and laughed and said, "Only now I begin to think I am fighting."

All the while, he was cutting and stabbing, jumping backward and forward, and all the while laughing. When he was dead, there were fifteen dead Crees lying around the earthen barrier. Then Low Horn's body was cut into small pieces and scattered all over the countryside to keep him from coming to life again.

III

That morning, before it was daylight, the two Blackfeet who had hidden in the willows left their hiding place and made their way home to the Blackfeet camp. When they got there, they told how Low Horn was surrounded by the Crees and how the firing had kept up through the night. As soon as Low Horn's father heard this, he got on his horse and rode through the camp, calling out, "My boy is surrounded. Let us all turn out and go help him. I have no doubt they are many tens to one, but he is powerful, and he may still be fighting."

No time was lost in getting ready, and soon a large war party started for the Cree camp. When they got there, the camp had already been moved. The father searched for his son's body, but it could only be found in small pieces, and not more than half of it could be gathered up.

After the fight was over, the Crees started on down toward their own country. One day, six Crees were

traveling along on foot, scouting far ahead. As they were going into a little ravine, a grizzly bear jumped up in front of them and ran after them. The bear overtook them and tore up five of them, one after another. The sixth got away and came back to camp. The Crees and the Blackfeet believe that this was the spirit of Low Horn. They think that he is still on the earth, but in a different shape.

Low Horn was killed about forty years ago. When he was killed, he was still a boy, not married, only about twenty-four years old.

Ghost Story

There was a camp, and in one of the lodges a little girl sat crying because she was angry. Her mother was doing everything she could to make her calm down. But at last the mother became angry herself, opened the lodge door, and pushed the little girl out, saying, "Ghost, take away this child."

A ghost must have been standing close by the door,

because when the mother put the little girl outside, something immediately picked her up and carried her off. There was no more crying. After a while, the woman went out but could not find her daughter. She went around to the other lodges, crying, looking for her child. But the girl could not be found anywhere.

The one who had taken the woman's daughter was a young ghost — a young ghost who lived with an old ghost — and when he got to his home, he brought the child in to the old one, saying, "Here is your food."

The next morning, the old ghost said to the little girl, "Go get me some firewood." So she went outside, and as she was gathering the wood, a little bird flew close to her and said, "You're getting that wood for yourself" — meaning that it was to be used to cook her.

When she brought the wood to the lodge, the old ghost looked at it and said, "This isn't the kind I want," and he sent her back to get some more. Again the little bird said to her, "You're getting that wood for yourself."

When the little girl returned to the lodge, the ghost complained again and sent her back to get a different kind of wood. So she went a third time, and again the bird spoke to her.

She was sent back a fourth time. Then the bird flew close to her and said, "This is the last time. When you go back, they'll cook you."

"It's no use," said the little girl. "The ghost has me in his power. What can I do?"

"I will help you," said the bird. "Do you see that high mountain peak right over there — the one that looks like a great lodge? I'll take you to it, and when you get there you must go up to the door in the rock and say:

Grandfather, save me
Father, save me
Brother, save me
Husband, save me.

That's what you must say at the door. You will see a big stone lying against the mountainside, right where I will take you, and that will be the door."

Then the bird told her to put her hands on its shoulders, and, flying close to the ground, it carried her up to the peak. When they got there, the girl repeated the magic words. Then the bird told her to put her hand on the rock and push it to one side. The door opened easily, and the girl went in. There was an old man sitting inside. "My grandchild, come in," he said. "I will protect you."

Now, when the old ghost saw that the little girl did not come back, he went out and followed her. He knew she had gone to the peak. As he got close, he began to hoot like an owl, and when he hooted the ground shook. Four times he hooted, and each time the ground shook.

When the child heard the ghost coming, she was afraid and ran around inside the lodge, trying to hide. But her grandfather told her to keep quiet and not to be afraid.

The ghost came and stood outside the door, saying, "Bring out my meat, or I'll come in and get it." Four times he said this.

"Come in and take her," answered the old man.

"Then you must open the door," said the ghost.

But not until he had been asked four times did the old man get up and pull open the door — just far enough for the ghost to get its head in. As the ghost started to come through, the old man let the door fly back and cut off the ghost's head, and the head fell on the ground inside.

Then the old man picked up the head and threw it outside. He said to the girl, "Get some dry wood and cover up this head." When she had covered it with wood, the old man set it on fire. Then he threw the ghost's body into the fire and handed the girl a stick and said, "Now, if anything rolls out, don't touch it with your hand. Push it back into the fire with this stick."

After the fire had burned for a while, the head and the body cracked open, and pieces of flint and old-time beads rolled out. The girl wanted to pick them up, but the old man said, "No, push them into the fire." Then they watched the fire until the ghost was all burned up.

Time passed, and when the girl reached the age of seventeen the old man said, "You may go back to your village." He dressed her like a man, made a robe for her, and painted it with red paint. He made her a thunder bow and put buffalo bull tails on the heels of her moccasins. Then he tied the skin of a prairie owl on her forehead.

"On your way home you will pass four villages," he said. "Stop at none of them. People will call out to you. But keep on going. After that you will come to a single lodge. Stop and go in, because by that time it will be nightfall, and there you will find an old woman who has great power: she kills people who come to her lodge. When you have gone inside, she will boil a kettle of brains and meal for you to eat. The brains will be those of someone she has killed. You must not eat this."

Then the old man gave the girl a live mink and told her to put it inside her robe on her breast. He said to her, "When the old woman gives you the bowlful of boiled brains, feed it to the mink.

Afterward, she will cook you some buffalo meat. Eat that."

Just before she was ready to leave, the old man told her that when she stopped at the old woman's lodge she must be careful not to go to sleep. "If you sleep," he said, "she will try to kill you. But if you do fall asleep, keep the mink up close to your neck, and it will be your guard."

So the girl set out on her journey, and as she came to the first village the women called out to her, "Come here, young man." But she paid no attention. When the women found that they could not attract her, they cried, "You walk like a woman!" This happened at each of the four villages.

Just at nightfall she came to the top of a hill, and down in the valley she saw a lone lodge. An old woman came out and said, "Come here, my grandchild." Then she took her by the hand and brought her down into the lodge. Before going in, the girl hung her thunder bow on the limb of a tree.

When she got inside, she found the lodge

equipped with the finest of everything. "My grandchild must be hungry," said the old woman. "I will cook you some mush." Then she put a pot of brains on the fire to cook.

As soon as it was ready, she handed it to her, and the girl pretended to eat — but fed it to the mink. "My grandchild is still hungry," said the old woman, and so she boiled some buffalo meat, which the girl ate.

After a while, the old woman asked the girl if she were sleepy. "Yes," said the girl, "I would like to sleep." And she lay down with the mink up close to her throat.

"I will sit up and keep the fire burning so that you will be warm," said the old woman. Then the girl pretended to sleep — but watched and saw the old woman move close to the fire and begin to scratch her leg. It grew larger. Then she crawled over to where the girl lay and raised her leg as though it were a club. But just as she held it over her head, the girl pushed the mink out. It caught hold of the woman's leg and tore off a piece of flesh.

The old woman cried out, "You've killed me!" and

fell over. Then she began to cry and said, "You have strong spirit-power."

The girl jumped up and ran out. But before she left she picked up a burning log and set the lodge on fire. Then she took her thunder bow and started off in the direction of her old camp.

She traveled all night, arriving at her village the next day. When she got there, she stood on a hill with her thunder bow, and the whole village came out to see this strange young man.

Then two young men came up to her and said, "Where did you come from?"

"This is my village," she replied. "I have been away a long time and have now come home." So they took her to the center of the camp and asked the crier to announce that a young man who belonged to the village had just arrived.

The crier called it through the camp, and everyone came out to look at her. But no one knew her. Finally they asked her who her family was. She hung her head

down, because it made her ashamed to remember that her mother had put her out of the lodge. At last she told them that she was the girl who had been thrown out-doors by her mother and carried off by the ghost.

Then they all recognized her, and her family took her to its lodge.

The Boy Who Was Sacrificed

Many years ago, in the Pawnee village on the Loup River, there lived a man who believed that if he sacrificed his son to *Ti-ra'-wa* it would be a blessing to him. He thought that if he did this thing, perhaps *Ti-ra'-wa* would speak to him face to face, and that he could talk to him just as two people would talk to one another, and that in this way he would learn many things that other people did not understand.

His son was a boy about ten years old, strong, growing up well, and the man loved him. It made him feel badly to think of killing him. He meditated long about this, but the more he thought about it, the more he believed that this sacrifice would please *Ti-ra'-wa*. There were many things that he wanted to understand and to do, and he thought that if he gave up his son these good things would come to him. So he decided to make the sacrifice.

One morning, he started out from the village and took the boy with him. When they got to the river, the man took his knife from its sheath, and as they were walking along he caught the boy by the shoulder and stabbed him quickly and cut him open.

When the boy was dead, he threw the body into the river and then went back to the village. When he got there, he went into his lodge and sat down. After a while, he said to his wife, "Where is the boy?" The woman said, "He went out with you when you went over to see the horses." The man answered, "No, I went out to where the horses are feeding and looked at them, but he did not go with me."

The man went out and pretended to look for the boy all through the village. At night, when the boy did not come home, the mother began to get frightened. For two days she hunted for the boy, and at last she got the old crier to call out from the top of the lodge and ask if anyone knew where he was. But none of the people had seen him.

Already the mother was mourning, and the father pretended to feel badly. No one could find the boy. Soon after this the tribe started on the summer hunt, and the father and mother went with them. The village made a good hunt, killing many buffalo, and made much dried meat.

Now, after the boy had been thrown into the river, he floated down with the current, turning over and over in the swift water. Sometimes he lay for a little while on a sand bar and then floated off again and was carried further downstream.

At last he came almost to the place where the whirlpool is, under the bluff where the medicine animals live. Two buzzards were sitting on the bluff, just above this place, and as they sat there, one of them stretched out his neck and looked up the river, and after he had looked, he said to the other, "I see a body."

Then both the buzzards flew down to where the boy was floating and got under him, and raised him on their backs, and lifted him out of the water. They flew up to the bluff, carrying the boy, and put him on the ground on top of the bluff over the big cave where the medicine animals have their lodge. In this lodge were all kinds of animals and all kinds of birds. There were bears, mountain lions, buffalo, elk, beaver, otter, deer —all kinds of animals, large and small, and all kinds of birds.

Just as the buzzards put the boy's body on the

ground, a messenger bird flew by. This is a bird smaller than a pigeon. Its back is blue, its breast is white, and its head is spotted. It flies quickly over the water, and when it sees a fish it dives down into the water to catch it. This bird is a servant, or messenger, for the medicine animals. When it saw what had happened, it flew down into the lodge and said, "There is a boy up on the hill. He is dead, and he is poor, and I want to have him brought to life again."

Then the bird told the medicine animals how the boy had been killed and how he had floated down the river — because the messenger bird knew all these things. When the bird had finished speaking, the medicine animals counseled together for a long time to decide what should be done, and each one made a speech, giving his opinion, but they could not make up their minds what ought to be done.

At last the question was given to four chiefs, who sat as judges to determine such matters after everything had been talked over. The judges thought for a while and then spoke together. Finally the chief of the judges said to the bird, "Messenger, we will not decide this question ourselves. You decide and say what shall be done."

The messenger was not long in deciding. He said, "I want this boy brought back to life." Then all the medicine animals stood up and went to where the boy lay and stood around him and prayed. At last the boy breathed, and then after a little while he breathed again, and at last he came to life and sat up. He opened his eyes and saw all the medicine animals standing around him, and he was amazed. He said to himself, "My father stabbed me and killed me, and now here I am in a great crowd of animals. What does this mean?" He could hardly believe what he saw.

Taking the boy with them, the medicine animals went back into the lodge. When they were all seated in the lodge, the four judges talked to each other, and the chief of the judges stood up and said, "Now, my people, we have brought this boy back to life, but he is poor, and we must do something for him. Let us teach him all

we know and make him one of us."

Then the medicine animals began to sing, and they danced. They taught the boy all their secrets. They taught him how to cut a man open and heal him, and how to shoot an arrow through a man and then cure him, and how to cut a man's tongue out and then put it back, and how to make a broken leg well again, and many other things.

When they had finished, they said to the boy, "We have brought you back to life and taught you all these things so that you can be one of us. Now you must stay with us one season. Your people have gone off on the summer hunt. You must stay here until autumn. Then you can go back to your people." So the boy stayed with the medicine animals in their lodge.

At last the people had returned from the hunt with plenty of dried meat. Then one day the animals said to the boy, "Your people have returned. Now you can go back to your village. Go and get lots of dried meat — the choicest pieces — and bring it to us here. We will have a feast."

The boy went home to the village. He got there in the night and went to his father's lodge. There was a little fire burning in the lodge. It was nearly out and gave only a little light, but he knew the place where his mother slept. He went up to her and put out his hand and touched her and pushed her a little. She awoke and sat up and looked at him, and he said, "I have come back."

When she saw him and heard him speak, she was very much surprised, and her heart was glad to see her boy again. She called to his father, and he woke up. When he saw the boy, he was afraid. He thought it was a ghost. The boy told them nothing of what had happened or where he had been. He just said, "I have come back."

In the morning all the people were surprised to hear that the boy had returned. They came and stood around him, looking at him and asking him questions. But he said nothing.

The next day the people still questioned him, and at last the boy said, "I have been all summer with friends, with people who have been good to me. I would like to take them a present of dried meat — the choicest pieces — so that we can have a feast."

The people said that this was good. They picked out four strong horses and loaded them with the meat. The boy's father gave some of it, and all the other people brought pieces and put them on the horses until they had big loads. They sent two young men with the boy to help him drive the horses. Then they started to go toward the bluff where the whirlpool is.

When they had almost reached the place, the boy sent the young men back to the village and went on alone, driving the horses in front of him. When he got to the home of the medicine animals, he unloaded the horses, turned them loose, and went into the lodge.

When the animals saw him, they all made a hissing noise to show they were glad he had come. The boy brought all the dried meat into the lodge, and they had a great feast.

After the feast, they had a doctors' dance, and the boy

was made a doctor, and again he was taught all that the medicine animals knew. After that he could do many wonderful things. He could sometimes go to a man who had been dead for a day and bring him back to life.

No one knew what the father had done. The boy never said anything to anyone. He knew that he could never have learned all these things unless his father had sacrificed him.

Wolf Man

There was once a man who had two bad wives. They had no shame. The man thought that if he went to a place where there were no other people he might teach these women to be good, so he moved his lodge far out on the prairie.

Near where they camped was a high butte, and every evening about sundown the man would climb up and look out over the countryside to see where the buffalo were feeding and if any enemies were coming. At the top of the butte there was a buffalo skull, and this is what the man would sit on.

"It's very lonesome here," said one of the women to the other, one day. "We have no one to talk to, no one to visit."

"Let's kill our husband," said the other. "Then we'll go back to our relatives and have a good time."

Early the next morning, the man went out to hunt as usual. As soon as he was out of sight, his wives went up on the butte and dug a deep pit and covered it over with thin sticks and grass and dirt. Then they put the buffalo skull on top.

In the afternoon, they saw their husband coming home, loaded down with all the meat he had killed. So they had to work fast to cook it for him before nightfall. After he had eaten, he went up on the butte and sat down on the skull the way he always did. But, just as he was settling himself, the thin sticks gave way, and he fell into the pit.

His wives were watching. When they saw him disappear, they took down the lodge, packed everything on the dog travois, and moved off, going toward the main camp. When they got close enough for people to hear, they began to cry and mourn.

"Why is this?" they were asked. "Why are you mourning? Where is your husband?"

"He is dead," they replied. "Five days ago he went out to hunt, and he never came back." Then they cried and mourned again.

Now, when the man fell into the pit, he was hurt. After a while he tried to get out, but he was so badly bruised he could not climb up. Just then a wolf passing by came alongside the pit and saw him and pitied him. He howled, *Ah-h-w-o-o-o-o!* and when the other wolves heard him they all came running to see what was the matter. Coyotes, badgers, and kit foxes came too.

"In this hole," said the wolf, "is my find. Here is a fallen-in man. Let us dig him out, and we will have him for our brother."

They all thought the wolf spoke well, and they began to dig. After a while they had a hole almost to where the man was. Then the wolf who had found him said, "Hold on! I want to speak a few words." The animals stopped and listened. "We will all have this man as our brother," said the wolf, "but I am the one who found him, so I think he should live with us wolves."

All the others said that this would be well. So the wolf went into the hole, and, breaking through the rest of the dirt, dragged out the almost dead man. They gave him a kidney to eat, and when he was able to walk a little the wolves took him to their home.

One of the wolves was very old and blind and had powerful medicine. He cured the man and made his head and hands look like the head and paws of a wolf. The rest of his body was not changed.

Now in those days the people used to make openings in the wall of the *pis'-kun* — where the buffalo meat was kept — and set snares to catch wolves and other animals when they came to steal meat. So one night when the wolves all went down to the *pis'-kun* to get meat, the wolf man said, "Stand back. I will go first and fix the snares so you won't be caught."

When the snares had been sprung, he called the wolves and all the others who had helped him — coyotes, badgers, and kit foxes — and they all went into the *pis'-kun* and feasted and took meat to carry home.

In the morning the people were surprised to find the meat gone and the nooses all drawn out. They wondered how it could have been done. For many nights the nooses were drawn and the meat stolen. But once, when the wolves came to steal, they found only the meat of a scabby bull. The wolf man was angry, and he cried out, *Ah-w-o-o-you-give-us-bad!*

The people heard him and said, "It's a wolf man who's done this! Now we'll catch him!" So the next day they put pemmican and nice back fat in the *pis'-kun* and hid close by. After dark the wolves came again, and when the wolf man saw the good food he ran to it and began eating. Then the people all rushed in and caught

him with ropes and took him to one of the lodges.

When they got inside to the light of the fire, they knew at once who it was. They said, "This is the man who was lost."

"No," said the man, "I was not lost. My wives tried to kill me. They dug a deep hole and I fell into it and was hurt so bad that I could not get out. But wolves took pity on me and helped me, or I would have died there."

When the people heard this, they were angry, and they told the man to do something.

"You say well," he replied. "I give those women to the chief and his men. They know what to do." And they did. And after that night the two women were never seen again.

Red Robe's Dream

Red Robe and Talking Rock were two young men growing up in the Blackfeet camp. As children, their life had been hard. Talking Rock was an orphan without any relatives, and Red Robe had only his grandmother.

This old woman worked hard. She tanned robes for hunters, made moccasins decorated with quills, and did everything she could to get a little food or worn-out robes to make clothes for the two boys.

When they grew to be twelve or thirteen years old, they began to do better. They herded horses and performed small services for the men who were well off. Sometimes they hunted and killed a little meat. For the work they did they were given three or four dogs, so that with the two dogs the old woman owned, they were able to pack their small lodge and other belongings when the camp moved, instead of carrying everything on their backs. After a while the boys were old enough to go out and fast. They had their dreams. Each found his secret helper who gave him power, and each became a warrior. Still they were poor compared with other young men of their age. They had bows but only a few arrows. They were not able to pay a medicine man to make shields for them. As yet they went to war only as servants.

Now, in this camp there was a beautiful girl named *Mā-min'*, and all the young men wanted to marry her. But Red Robe wanted her more than the rest. Her father was a rich medicine man who never invited anyone to feast with him except chiefs and great warriors, and Red Robe rarely entered his lodge. He used to dress as well as he could and stand for a long time near the door, watching to see if the young woman would come out. Whenever they met, he thought the look she gave him was friendly.

But wherever *Mā-min'* went, her mother or some woman of the family went with her. So Red Robe could never speak to her, though he was often nearby. One day, while she was gathering wood for the lodge, and her mother was out of sight behind a clump of brush, Red Robe walked up to her. He took her hands in his, and she did not try to draw them away.

"I am poor, very poor," he said, "and it is useless to ask your father to let me marry you. He will only say no. But let us go away from here — far away. We will find a tribe that will be good to us."

"I cannot do what you ask," she said. "I cannot go away and leave my mother to cry for me. Let us wait. Go to war. Do something great. Then perhaps it will not be useless if you ask my father to give me to you."

Red Robe said nothing. He waited.

A few days later, Three Bulls, chief of the camp, asked the medicine man for his daughter *Mā-min'*.

Three Bulls had several wives and many children, some of them grown and married. There were gray hairs on his head, and his face had begun to show wrinkles. No one thought that he would take another wife. So when the news spread through the camp, people were surprised.

But the medicine man did not dare refuse. Three Bulls had a fierce temper, and when he spoke, people hurried to do what he said. He never talked loud or called anyone a bad name. When someone refused to do what he ordered, he only smiled and then killed the person. He was brave. In battle with enemies he was the equal of twenty men, rushing here, there, into the thickest of the fight and killing—always with a smile on his face.

That day Red Robe had planned to start with a war party. But when he heard the news he asked his friend Talking Rock to take word to the leader that he had changed his mind and would not go. He asked his friend to stay with him instead of joining the war party, and Talking Rock said, "Yes, I will stay with you." Then Red Robe went down to the stream by himself and waited.

As he had expected, *Mā-min'* soon came for a skin of water. He took her hands, as he had done before, and began to beg her to go away with him. The girl cried bitterly but did not know what to say.

The two were standing in plain sight of the camp, and someone went to the chief's lodge and told him what was happening.

"Go to the spring," said the chief, "and tell that boy to let the young woman go. She is to be my wife."

The person did as he was told, but the two

young people paid no attention to him. Then Three Bulls quietly walked up to them and stabbed the young man with a flint-pointed lance. As Red Robe fell dying at her feet, *Mā-min'* looked down for an instant, then turned and ran to her father's lodge.

"Bring wood," the chief called out. "Let everyone bring wood—all you have in your lodges."

The people hurried to obey. What Three Bulls ordered was soon done, because the whole camp feared him, and soon a great pile of wood was heaped beside the dead man.

The chief lifted the body, placed it on the pile of wood, and told a woman to bring coals and set fire to the pile. When this had been done, the people went back to their lodges, all except Three Bulls, who kept poking the fire until it was burned out and no wood or trace of a human body was left. Nothing remained except a little pile of ashes, and these he scattered.

Still he was not satisfied. Something warned him. Now he ordered that the lodges be taken down, that everything be packed up, and that the trail of the moving camp should pass over the pile of ashes.

Some time before this, when Red Robe had made his long fast and his dream had come to him, he had returned to his grandmother's lodge and had told his friend Talking Rock what had been said to him by the dream.

"If I die," he said, "and you are near, do not leave me. Go to the place where I fell, and if my body has been destroyed, look carefully. If you can find even a shred of my flesh or a piece of my bone, it will be well."

Then he said, "Here are four arrows that the dream told me to make. If you can find a part of my body, flesh or bone, or even hair, cover it with a robe, and standing over it, shoot three arrows one after another into the air, and each time say, 'Look out!' When you shoot the fourth arrow say, 'Look out, Red Robe, the arrow will hit you!' and as you say this, turn and run away without looking back. If you do this just as I have told you, I will live again."

As the camp moved, Three Bulls stood and watched it passing over the place where the fire had been. He saw the ashes scattered by the trailing ends of the lodge poles and travois and by the feet of many people and dogs.

Still he was not satisfied, and for a long time after the last of the people had passed he remained there. Then he went on across the flat and up over a ridge. But after a while he returned, once, twice, four times, to the top of the hill and looked back at the place where the camp had been. At last he felt sure that no one remained, and he went on.

But Talking Rock was there. He had been hiding in the brush all the while, watching the chief. When he saw him disappear for the last time, he waited a while longer. Then he came out and began to search through the dust where the fire had been.

All morning and far into the afternoon, Talking Rock swept the dust this way and that, turning it over and over, in a circle that kept growing wider. At last, just as he was about to give up, he found a small piece of charred bone.

Taking off his robe, he covered the piece of bone as he had been told to do and even raised the robe along its middle, making it look as if it covered a person. Then he shot three of the arrows into the air, each time saying, "Look out!"

Then he took the fourth arrow, shot it, and cried, "Look out, Red Robe, the arrow will hit you!" and turning, he ran as fast as he could.

He wanted to look back, but he didn't dare. On and on he ran, and then, at last, behind him he heard the sound of running feet. A hand gripped his shoulder, and a voice said, "Why so fast, my friend?"

Stopping and turning, he found himself face to face with Red Robe. He could not believe what he saw and had to hold his friend hard in his arms before he knew that this was real.

The camp had not moved far. Following the trail, the

two friends arrived soon after dark and went to the old grandmother's lodge. At first the poor woman could not believe her eyes. But then her grandson spoke, and she held him in her arms and cried.

Then he said to her, "Grandmother, go to the chief's lodge and tell him that I, Red Robe, need dried meat."

The old woman hesitated, but Red Robe said, "Go, do not be afraid. Three Bulls is now the one who will be afraid."

When the old woman entered the great lodge, the chief turned and looked at her. "Red Robe sent me," she said. "He wants dried meat." Of those who were in the lodge, only Three Bulls showed no surprise. "It is what I expected," he said. "He lives again, and I can do nothing." Turning to his wives he said, "Give her meat."

"Did you see *Mā-min'?*" asked Red Robe, when his grandmother had returned with the meat and had told him what the chief had said.

"No, she was not in the lodge, but two women were

approaching as I left. I think they were the girl and her mother."

"Go back once more," he said, "and tell Three Bulls to send me that young woman."

But now the poor grandmother was afraid. "I don't dare tell him that," she cried. "He would kill us both."

"Do not be afraid," said Red Robe. "My power is greater than his. He is as weak and helpless as an old bull spending his last days before the wolves pull him down."

The grandmother went to the lodge and told the chief what Red Robe wanted. *Mā-min'* was there, her head covered with her robe. The chief told her to get up and go with the old woman. Slowly at first, then breaking into a run, she went to the lodge where Red Robe was waiting. With a cry, she threw herself into his arms.

They were married then, and their happiness was great. They always had plenty. Red Robe became a chief. They were given long life. They were never sick.

When they were very old, one morning their children said, "Awake! Rise and eat." They did not move. In the night, in sleep, without pain, their shadows had gone into the hills.

Guide to Special Terms

A-wa-heh' (a-wah-HAY), a Blackfeet expression meaning "Take courage," or "Be strong."

Blackfeet (singular or plural), a tribe formerly of eastern Montana and southern Saskatchewan, now on reservation lands in western Montana. Also called Blackfoot (singular, the plural is Blackfoot or Blackfeet).

butte (BYOOT), a steep, usually treeless hill in desert or prairie country.

Comanche (kom-ANN-chee), a Texas tribe.

coup (KOO), a French word (introduced by French explorers) meaning "strike" or "blow," used in the expression "to count *coup,*" to strike, or touch, an enemy in combat.

Cree, a central Canadian tribe, traditional enemy of the Blackfeet.

Kom-in'-a-kus (kom-IN-ah-koose), literally "Round," a Blackfeet man's name.

Mā-min' (may-MIN), literally "Wing," a Blackfeet woman's name.

Pawnee, a tribe formerly of Kansas and Nebraska, now on reservation lands in Oklahoma.

pemmican, a preserved food made of lean pounded meat and melted fat, sometimes with berries added.

pis'-kun (PISS-kun), the Blackfeet term for the large brushwood enclosure used to trap buffalo. Carcasses waiting to be butchered were often kept in the *pis'-kun*.

Ti-ra'-wa (tee-RAH-wah), the supreme power worshipped by the Pawnee.

travois (TRA-voy, with the "a" as in the English word "travel"), a French term (introduced by French explorers) for the typical vehicle used by Plains Indians: a pair of poles strapped to the sides of a horse or dog and dragged with a load tied between the poles directly behind the animal.

wu hu is tat' tan (woo-huh-is-TOT-tahn), the Cheyenne term for human being.

Story Sources

Grinnell's most important collections of Indian stories are *Blackfoot Lodge Tales: The Story of a Prairie People* (Charles Scribner's Sons, 1892), *By Cheyenne Campfires* (Yale University Press, 1926), and *Pawnee Hero Stories and Folk-Tales with Notes on the Origin, Customs and Character of the Pawnee People* (Forest and Stream Publishing Co., 1889). All three have been reissued in paperbound editions by the University of Nebraska Press. Grinnell's *Blackfeet Indian Stories* (Charles Scribner's Sons, 1913) is essentially a young reader's edition of *Blackfoot Lodge Tales* (see above), with several stories omitted and five new ones added. Further tales collected by

Grinnell were published in *Journal of American Folklore* between 1893 and 1921. Five more, including two Bluejay stories from the Northwest Coast, appeared in *Harper's Monthly Magazine* during the years 1900 and 1901.

Sources for the nine stories in the present collection are as follows: "The Whistling Skeleton," *Blackfoot Lodge Tales*, p. 70; "Sees in the Night," *By Cheyenne Campfires*, p. 83; "Deer Boy," *Pawnee Hero Stories and Folk-Tales*, p. 182; "The Stolen Girl," *Cheyenne*, p. 129; "The Death of Low Horn," *Blackfoot*, p. 82; "Ghost Story," *Cheyenne*, p. 157; "The Boy Who Was Sacrificed," *Pawnee*, p. 161; "Wolf Man," *Blackfoot*, p. 78; "Red Robe's Dream," *Blackfeet Indian Stories*, p. 130.

Suggestions for Further Reading

Colorful descriptions of Pawnee and Blackfeet life are included in Grinnell's *Pawnee Hero Stories* and in his *Blackfoot Lodge Tales* (see Story Sources, above). Up-to-date articles on all the Plains tribes will be found in volume thirteen of the forthcoming *Handbook of North American Indians,* to be published by the Smithsonian Institution. The books listed below are nontechnical and readily available.

Erdoes, Richard, *The Sun Dance People: The Plains Indians, Their Past and Present*, Alfred A. Knopf, New York, 1972. A young reader's history of the Plains Indians from the nineteenth century to the present.

Ewers, John C., *The Blackfeet: Raiders on the Northwestern Plains*, University of Oklahoma Press, Norman, Okla., 1958.

Grinnell, George Bird, *The Cheyenne Indians: Their History and Ways of Life*, 2 vols., University of Nebraska Press, Lincoln, Nebr., 1972. The standard account of Cheyenne culture.

———, *The Fighting Cheyennes*, University of Oklahoma Press, Norman, Okla., 1977. A history of the Cheyenne wars as told by Cheyenne warriors.

Lowie, Robert H., *Indians of the Plains*, American Museum Science Books, Natural History Press, Garden City, N.Y., 1963.

Rachlis, Eugene, and Ewers, John C., *Indians of the Plains*, American Heritage Publishing Co., New York, 1960. Profusely illustrated, written for young readers.

Schultz, J.W., *My Life as an Indian*, Fawcett World Library, New York, no date. First-hand account of life among the Blackfeet by an associate of George Bird Grinnell.

APR 2 '90